CONTENTS

D1811204

CHAPTER

	Introduction	4
1	This is Television	5
2	The Bulletin	13
3	Start Filming and We'll Give You a Story	21
4	Banned!	29
5	Reveal Your Sources	41
6	The Interview	49
7	"You're Biased!"	57
8	On Air!	63

INTRODUCTION

Television news is the most powerful of the news media.

Think of the assassination of President Kennedy; or of human kind's first steps on the moon; or of the Falklands War; or of America winning back the America's Cup at Perth; or of Margaret Thatcher's third election victory; or of the Zeebrugge ferry disaster.

And you think of pictures, the pictures you have seen on television.

Television can educate, influence, entertain, upset, bore. But the television news journalist is trying to do only one thing: *inform*.

In the course of his career he will fall foul of the authorities, he will be accused of bias, he will be challenged as to where he got his information. People will try to convince him there is a story when he knows there isn't one, or there isn't a story when he knows there is.

The aim of this small book is to outline some of the pressures the television journalist is subject to, some of the hurdles he will have to clear, and some of the traps he will have to avoid to get his story ''on the air''.

THIS IS TELEVISION

Let's start by stating the obvious: television news is *pictures*. This, above all, is what sets it apart from radio news, newspapers, news magazines, news letters, news anything. And pictures form the single raw element which will dominate the television news journalist's life.

"It's a great story...", "I know that, but what picture have we got?"; "We're short of picture on this story, send a crew out to shoot some general stuff..."; "Need more picture? Get on to the picture library and see if we've covered this sort of thing before...".

Classic snippets of television newsroom conversation. And not the sort of talk you hear in any other kind of newsroom. What matters most, of course, is the strength of the story itself.

But take the story from the moment it breaks. Reports are coming in of a fire in a London underground station. Newsrooms across London leap into action. Reporters are dispatched by their news editors to the scene. The radio reporter grabs his tape recorder. The newspaper reporter grabs his notebook. The television reporter grabs his camera crew (or vice versa). For the duration of the story they will barely leave each other's side. And when the result of their efforts comes to be judged, that judgment will be made on the strength of the pictures the team shot.

"Did they get the shots that told the story?" "Did they get the important interviews?" "Did they miss any important action?" These are the questions which will be asked back at base.

Pictures may set television news apart from other forms of journalism, but they need words to describe them. And words are what every branch of journalism has in common. But words are a different tool for a television journalist than they are for his colleagues in other branches of the profession.

First of all, he must learn to **write to picture** (in television, people say "picture" rather than "pictures"). What a television reporter should never do is write his story without regard to the picture available. On the contrary, his task is to marry the two elements, which together constitute the shape of his story. "Writing to picture" is not something you can be taught; there are no hard and fast rules about it. Rather it should be second nature. I have known television journalists give up the job and move to newspapers, because they are not happy to write to picture — they find it gets in the way of what they are trying to say.

Fine. But a television journalist relishes his picture, and enjoys writing to it. A good television journalist will never describe in his commentary exactly what the picture is showing. That is talking down to the viewer. Nor will he ever "talk against" the picture — i.e. describe something totally different to what the viewer is seeing. That is confusing. And, possibly his most difficult skill, he will know when to say nothing at all, and let the picture tell the story. He will never use words when he doesn't need to.

And he will never say, as I have just done several times, "never". Because, to repeat, there are no rules.

Yet it can be so easy to get it wrong. A TV news bulletin in Britain once carried a story about a baby elephant being born at London Zoo. The final shot showed the baby, together with the young girl who was its keeper. Over this shot, the newscaster read, "Mother and baby are doing well."

How should a television journalist go about writing to picture? He should watch the picture editor edit the piece, then he should make a **shotlist** — a description of every shot, with its exact timing. He should write to the list, then read his commentary against the picture to make sure it works.

What do Walt and Amy Bergman of Springfield, Illinois, USA; Fred and Ethel Bloggs of Derby, England; and Bruce and Sheila Patterson of Sydney, Australia, have in common? They are all typical, average viewers. And that means they are the viewers the television journalist reports for. And here his role differs markedly from that of the newspaper journalist.

Whether in the United States, Britain, or Australia, a newspaper knows within broad parameters who its readers are and it aims specifically at them.

Record a news report on video, make a shotlist for it, write a commentary, and then read it to the picture. See how successful you are at making your commentary fit the picture.

Take Britain. We all know, as the famous advert used to say, that "Top people take *The Times*". We also know what that means, however general it may sound. It means lawyers, doctors, teachers, civil servants, clergymen . . . We also know, again in the most general terms, what kind of people read the *Sun.* In general it's the working man who likes a bit of spice with his news.

In Britain the distinction between the two types of newspaper is highlighted by the words "heavies" and "tabloids". The former refers to the more serious type of newspaper — *The Times, Independent, Financial Times, Guardian, Telegraph* —while tabloids (a printing term actually denoting the size of the newspaper) refers to the more popular, racier kind of newspaper, where the accent is more on entertainment than news — the *Sun, Mirror, Star, Mail, Express.*

There is another point too, although this tends to be more true in Britain than in, say, the United States. The newspapers are openly political. The *Telegraph*, for instance, takes a political stance in favour of the Conservative Party. The *Mirror* supports the Labour Party. Most major national papers will — again in very broad terms — support a political party. This was made particularly clear when a new newspaper was launched in Britain called *The Independent.* It chose the name precisely to distinguish itself from those British newspapers with overt political affiliations.

So, the buyer of a newspaper knows what he wants, and he knows what he will get. Look, by contrast, at the television viewer.

Who is he? He might be a Harvard or Oxford professor. He might be a Senator or Member of Parliament. He might be a musician, a professional footballer, a chef, a pop singer, a criminal, or unemployed. And what of his politics? He might be Republican or Democrat, Conservative or Labour, he might be a revolutionary Marxist-Leninist, an anarchist, or he might never give a moment of his time to political thought.

And he might, of course, be all of these things. Around 20 million people watch ABC's *World News Tonight* every night in the United States. Around 10 million watch ITN's *News at Ten* in Britain. That is as many people as buy every national newspaper in each country put together, and more. It is simply too large a number to categorize.

There is a technical distinction, too, that sets television apart from newspapers, and which the reporter must never lose sight of. You can read the

Read a newspaper article only once. Then test yourself to see how many facts you remember.

newspaper from cover to cover, then you can read it again.

Not so on television. Watch a televison news bulletin and you get only one chance to understand it. (The video recorder means that need not necessarily be true, but the television journalist does not let that enter his

thinking: not every viewer will have a recorder, and not every video owner will use it.)

So what effect does this have on the television journalist? It means he must report in such a way that the viewer never has to say, "What? I didn't understand that". And it does not matter what the report is about.

It means not using difficult words like "propitious" or "apposite", even if they are exactly the right words in a particular context. It means not using sentences like this one, which, although grammatically quite correct, and syntactically within the bounds of usage, weave their way, in a certain sense, through various sub-clauses, notwithstanding the fact that the longer they get, the more complicated they become, until, finally, they lose themselves in a tangled web of verbiage . . . and Amy Bergman, Ethel Bloggs and Sheila Patterson will all have gone into the kitchen to make a cup of tea.

A bulletin that is strictly impartial, that the university professor will understand without labelling it banal, that the poorly educated viewer will understand without feeling that he is being patronized, that tells the stories in a straightforward, uncomplicated and interesting way . . . that's Television.

THE BULLETIN

Take two of the most watched television news bulletins in the western world: ABC of America's *World News Tonight* which has an average nightly audience of up to 20 million, and ITN of Britain's *News at Ten*, which has an average nightly audience of up to 10 million.

World News Tonight is the flagship news bulletin of the American TV network, American Broadcasting Company (ABC). It is transmitted every night during the week at 7 pm. Eastern Standard Time (with other transmission times for other time zones).

If you look at the television listings in your newspaper to see what time ABC's *World News Tonight* begins, and what time it ends, the listing will inform you quite simply that the news begins at 7 pm and ends at 7.30 pm. Half an hour of prime-time television given to the news. And as far as you, the viewer, are concerned, that's exactly what it is: a news programme which lasts for half an hour.

But for the television journalist it's not like that at all. ABC's *World News Tonight* begins at 7 pm, just as the newspaper says. But between 7 pm and 7.30 pm there are four commercial breaks, which together total 6 minutes and 10 seconds. And the programme actually ends at 28 minutes and 28 seconds past 7 pm. Subtract 6 minutes and 10 seconds from 28 minutes and 28 seconds, and you are left with 22 minutes and 18 seconds.

The 'net' running time of ABC's *World News Tonight*, then, is nowhere near the half-hour it appears to be from the television listings.

Let's look now at *News at Ten*, the flagship news programme of Britain's Independent Television Network. *News at Ten* is produced by the news division of that network, Independent Television News (ITN).

Once again, if you turn to the television listings in the newspapers, you will see that *News at Ten* begins at 10 pm and ends at 10.30 pm, and is therefore, from the viewer's point of view, a half-hour news programme. It does indeed start at 10 pm, but there is a single commercial break of 2 minutes and 40 seconds, and the programme actually ends at 29 minutes and 10 seconds past 10 pm. Do the subtraction and you end up with a 'net' running time for *News at Ten* of 26 minutes and 30 seconds.

If it comes as any kind of surprise to learn how precise these figures are, then it has to be understood that

Time your national TV news with a stopwatch: compare the real running time with the newspaper listing.

precision is intrinsic to the nature of television news. It is the name of the game. You must not be even one second out either way when it comes to compiling a bulletin.

And if you think that it must be impossible to be so precise, because it means someone sitting with a stop-watch, timing every word, and how on earth can you be sure the newscaster will read at exactly the right speed, and what if he has a coughing fit, or sneezes, or loses his place, or stutters, and what if it goes wrong, and anyway no-one can possibly do anything to the exact second, it just can't work like that . . .

. . . then all I can say to you is, you are absolutely right on every count. It *does* mean someone sitting there with a stop-watch, and it *is* impossible, and newscasters *do* sometimes sneeze, and yes it's true that people just *don't* live to the exact second, except sprinters.

And television journalists. For the television journalist *timing* is of the essence. It influences every decision he makes. Whereas a newspaper journalist talks in terms of word numbers ("Write me a 250 word piece"; "I can give you 500 words"; "The story's worth 750"), the television journalist always refers to timings — "I can take a minute 45, no more"; "I've got a lot of good material, let me have two-and-a-quarter"; "OK it's an epic, you can go up to three".

If, after discussion with the programme editor, the reporter agrees to put together a report at a minute 40, and he then produces one at a minute 45, he will cause the editor problems. I once heard an editor say to a reporter who had turned in a piece ten seconds longer than agreed "What the hell are you playing at? No-one asked you to remake Ben Hur!"

There has to be a guideline (no "rules", remember) and it is that in television news you speak at the rate of three words to the second. No-one can deliberately and consistently speak at that rate, and words differ in length. But if you average it out over the length of the programme, that is how it works out. So when the bulletin is being prepared, when scripts and reports are checked for their length, that is the rate at which timings are calculated.

Timing is the mechanics of television news. It is the element which gives a news bulletin cohesion and shape. And it imposes a particular discipline on all those who work in the medium. That discipline starts at the top, with the programme editor, and it works its way down. Ultimately it touches every journalist who works on

the programme.

But how can you put the news across in 22 minutes and 18 seconds? If you really wanted to report everything of significance which had happened in the world on any given day, it would take hours and hours. Yet for the programme editor of *World News Tonight*, there are just 22 minutes and 18 seconds available; and for his *News at Ten* counterpart the slightly more generous 26 minutes and 30 seconds.

You use your **news judgment,** that's how you do it. News judgment is not something you can learn from a book. It is practically impossible to be either totally right or totally wrong in making a news judgment.

If, on the same day, a gunman runs amok in a quiet town in England and shoots dead 15 people, and the British Prime Minister resigns because of, say, a financial scandal, which story would you use to lead the bulletin?

As a television journalist, there are a number of factors which would influence your decision: what picture is there available? do we have a reporter at the scene? have we got the important interviews?

It is a difficult choice. The shooting story is undoubtedly the more dramatic. But the resignation of the Prime Minister will certainly have a more

Note the order of stories in a bulletin. Do you agree with the editor's choice?

important effect on the British people. Only one thing is certain: whichever decision you make, you cannot be accused of being categorically wrong. There can be no right and wrong way of doing it. At the end of the day, the programme editor makes the decision on the basis of his news judgment, his "feel" for a story.

The kind of news judgment or perspective exercised by the programme editor is broad in nature: he is comparing one story with another, one set of events with another, and thinking always of the right place in the bulletin for a particular story.

The news judgment exercised by a reporter in the field will be narrower in perspective. He will be covering a particular story and trying to assess its importance. It can be tricky.

In my early days as a reporter, I covered a political demonstration in the north of England at which fighting

broke out. Police on horseback charged to break up the demonstrators. I had never seen such a thing before. I telephoned the programme editor and described it in terms which would have been more appropriate to World War Three. News judgment — perspective — comes only one way: with experience. And that experience teaches a reporter not only how to judge better his own story, but to remember that his is only one of perhaps 20 stories which will run in the news bulletin.

News is *relative*. A story has its intrinsic worth, but that worth is relative to the other stories that are happening that day. And the intrinsic worth of a story can diminish as new and better stories come in.

But when all the judgments have been made, when the second hand of the clock approaches air time, when the production assistant in the control room says: Ten seconds to air, nine, eight, seven, six . . .'', the end product goes before the public. The Bulletin.

Yet even then it is not a concrete commodity. News does not stop happening when a news bulletin goes on the air. The newscaster wears an earpiece into which the programme team in the control room can talk. Changes are frequently made on air, as new stories come in and others are dropped. A news programme is always live, and it often shows.

A programme editor will spend all day shaping his programme, then halfway through the programme word reaches him that an attempt has been made on the life of the President of the United States. He throws everything else out of the window.

Most changes are smaller and more subtle than that. A word change here or there, or an update on a particular story. Or a major new story may have broken an hour before airtime, giving the production team time to alter the bulletin.

Not until one particular moment can the programme editor of *News at Ten* relax: 29 minutes and 11 seconds past 10 pm.

"START FILMING AND WE'LL GIVE YOU A STORY"

It's the classic dilemma of the television journalist. How do you avoid creating the news that you are supposed to be reporting?

Northern Ireland in the 1970s was not an easy story to report. High tensions, a volatile atmosphere, anger, frustration, hurt. Emotions made manifest in mass demonstrations, violence and murder. In amongst it all were the television reporters and their camera crews.

I have chosen Northern Ireland to illustrate this chapter, because it is the perfect example of how news can become distorted, either unwittingly, or because some people set out to distort it.

The present "troubles" began in the late 1960s and of course are not over yet. There are still mass demonstrations, barricades still burn and bodies are still found on lonely country roads.

But the nature of the story has changed, and the way it is reported has changed correspondingly. And — crucially — the actors in the drama have changed. Most of them were not born, or were children, in the late 1960s.

When anger spills out on to the streets, it must have a target. Its real target is very often something intangible, and quite possibly a long way away. The anti-Vietnam war demonstrations in the United States in the 1960s were directed against Washington and the White House. But they took place in San Francisco, Chicago, New York, Kent State University, and so on.

The target the demonstrators will pick, though, is the nearest tangible one. That is usually the police or the army, which represent the visible manifestation of the authority the demonstrators don't like.

When the British army moved into Northern Ireland in 1972, it gave the demonstrators a very real target. The extremist Catholics wanted Britain to give up Northern Ireland as a province, and here were the armed forces of Britain, sent to enforce an order those Catholics refused to acknowledge.

The national television news teams were also sent across the water. They, too, quickly became targets for the crowd's anger.

In the early 1970s, while I was a television news writer but not yet a reporter, our reporters and crews would return to base after stints in Northern Ireland with horror stories of being chased by the crowds, being attacked and beaten up, and of having camera gear smashed.

But as the 1970s progressed, elements among the protesters began to see the value of having television on the scene. If television could show them in a bad light, it could also show them in — by their definition — a "good" light. "If we have a point to put across to the government in London, what more effective way to do it than to use television?"

"Use" television. It sends shudders through the television journalist. Sometimes he *cannot* avoid it. When Buddhist monks burned themselves to death in protest against the Vietnam war, they were using the cameras. They knew that their actions would be recorded and reported, and correspondingly announced their intentions in advance. It would have had no impact at all to have carried out their act in the middle of the night in a field miles from anywhere, with no-one any the wiser. But an act as dramatic as that cannot be ignored by the news media.

Sometimes the reporter *does not* want to avoid it. After a string of child murders in Atlanta in the early 1980s, the police appealed to the public to come forward with information. They issued descriptions of the wanted man

23

to the public. How did they do it? There is only one way: through the media.

Sometimes the reporter *should* avoid it. In the Biafran war in the 1960s, television cameras filmed a senior army officer shooting dead a prisoner with his hands tied behind his back. There was international outrage. The Nigerian government, as a result, ordered the officer to be arrested and shot. He insisted that the camera teams should film his execution. They did.

Sometimes the reporter *can* avoid it. Northern Ireland again. Late evening, after a rally in a Republican area of town. The police had warned of predictable violence, after the emotive speeches to the crowd. They were out in force, so was the army, so were the television cameras. It didn't happen.

The rowdier elements were clearly annoyed that the ritual stone-throwing and barricade-burning had not taken place. But the camera crews were still there. It was a difficult situation to judge. The atmosphere was still volatile. Was it safe to leave the scene?

It was dark. If there was to be any filming, the teams would have to switch their lights on. A group of young men approached the ITN camera crew. "Switch on your lights and we'll give you a riot," said their leader. The crews smiled at each other. At last they knew they could safely leave because there was no story.

It can happen in reverse. When television cameras filmed a mob in Belfast attacking a car with two soldiers inside, dragging the soldiers from the car and taking them away to kill them, leaders in the mob knew that the pictures could help the police identify them.

They tried to take as much of the film off the cameramen as possible, and threatened all the cameramen there — television as well as photographers — that if the pictures were published, their lives would be at risk.

In other words, the exact converse of "start filming and we'll give you a story". The pictures, of course, were published.

Sometimes they *must* avoid it. An American television team were once seen to hand money to rioters in Belfast to encourage them to hurl firebombs at police and soldiers, so the cameraman could get good pictures. If journalists were allowed to punish their colleagues for unethical behaviour, that team would have got life imprisonment.

The culprit every time, of course, is *picture* — that element that sets television news apart from other forms of journalism. Picture is powerful, and the fact that television can broadcast it to millions makes it all the more so. And, therefore, all the more desirable to someone who wants to put a message across.

Twenty years after the latest troubles began in Northern Ireland, the demonstrations still exist, but they have changed in nature. There are still the set-piece demonstrations, but they are fewer. Now the demonstrations are more political in tone. But television still plays its role.

When, in 1987, Protestant leaders in Northern Ireland decided to break into

Watch several news bulletins. See if you can tell which of the events reported were deliberately organized to make news and attract the cameras, and which were spontaneous.

a meeting in Stormont Castle, to register their opposition to the Anglo-Irish Agreement, they made absolutely sure that the television teams knew in advance.

The television teams knew that the event was staged for the cameras. But there was also a further point to consider. The Protestants involved had frequently — and volubly — voiced their opposition to the Anglo-Irish Agreement. This was another way of showing it, and therefore a valid news story.

It is a thin line, though, between that and offering to stage a riot. Those extremists too would argue they were simply voicing their opposition. Where do you draw the line? Once again, there are no rules.

What are the alternatives? In the mid-1970s the then Government Minister for Northern Ireland asked the television news teams not to cover events in Northern Ireland for a time, to see if that would help keep the violence down.

The journalists refused. What is the difference between that and **censorship**? If the press had agreed on that occasion, who was to tell when the government might make a similar request again? And what if that request then became an order?

In 1980 I tried to cover the shipyard

If you were the editor of a television news programme, what criteria would you use to decide whether or not to cover an event which had been set up to attract media attention?

strikes in Poland, as the free trade union Solidarity grew in strength. My crew and I were arrested twice and then expelled from the country. That is censorship.

True television news can only exist in a free society. Indeed, if you want to know whether a particular country has a truly free society, send a tele-vision news team there, and see what happens when, in the centre of the capital, the cameraman lifts his camera from the boot of his car and puts it on his shoulder.

And true television news can only exist when the decision on whether or not to cover a story is the journalist's and the journalist's alone. But even a free society is sometimes not quite as free as it may seem . . .

BANNED!

In the United States, arguably the freest country in the world when it comes to censorship, a local authority banned as pornographic a book entitled *Make it with Mademoiselle*. It turned out to be a sewing manual.

In Britain it has been a crime for nearly 80 years to report the number of cups of tea drunk each week in a Government Department. If a journalist reported the details of a new carpet in a Government Minister's office, he was breaking the law.

Censorship affects all the media and will always sooner or later lead to absurdity, because of its very nature. Censorship is like a net — you always catch a lot of things beside the fish you are after.

In Britain the net is called the Official Secrets Act. Section Two of the act made it an offence for any person in government service, past or present, to disclose any information he had obtained owing to his position. It was also – and this is the part which affected the journalist – an offence to receive such information.

On two of the occasions on which the British Government invoked the

Act in the 1980s, the results were notorious and far-reaching. In the first instance it lost outright. In the second the Government's action caused derision in Britain and Australia, was defeated in the Australian courts, and was finally defeated in the highest appeal court in Britain.

The first instance involved a government employee (civil servant) called Clive Ponting. In 1985 he was accused of an offence under Section Two of the Official Secrets Act. The allegation was that he had passed papers on the sinking of the Argentine warship *General Belgrano* in the Falklands War to a Member of Parliament.

If proven, it was a clear-cut breach of the Official Secrets Act. The judge certainly considered it proven. He told the jury that the act protected, "The policies of the state . . . the policies laid down by those recognized organs of government and authority", and he directed the jury that Clive Ponting had broken the act.

Clive Ponting was so convinced he would be found guilty, that on the morning of the verdict his wife had brought him a suitcase of clothes to take with him to prison. The jury ignored the judge's advice and acquitted Clive Ponting. This verdict tore a pretty big hole in the censorship net.

Only a year later, the British Government became embroiled again. It all began when a retired officer of MI5 (the secret service agency dealing with internal security in the UK) named Peter Wright decided to publish his memoirs in a book called *Spycatcher*. The British Government claimed this was in breach of the Official Secrets Act, because Mr Wright, like all civil servants, had signed a document when he entered the Government's employ promising to abide by the Act, which meant not divulging details of his work.

The problem for the British Government was that Mr Wright lived in Tasmania, which meant they could not prosecute him for breach of the act. Instead they had to challenge his right to publish by taking him to court in Australia.

Their further problem was that the judge hearing the case made it quite clear early on that he thought the British Government was behaving in a thoroughly unreasonable way, and no-one was surprised when he ruled against them and in favour of Mr Wright. His ruling was later upheld in the Australian Supreme Court.

But by now the British rights to Mr Wright's book had been secured, and excerpts were being published in a British newspaper. And so the British

Government took action in the British courts to prevent publication of the book, and of extracts from it, in Britain. They won.

Until now the Government's actions and the court rulings had only applied to the book and the newspaper which had secured serial rights. Now, suddenly, all the press, including television, became involved.

In July 1987 the Law Lords, the highest court in the land, imposed a blanket ban on all forms of publication of Mr Wright's book, whether in book form or in newspapers. They also banned *all* reporting of the case, which by this stage was before the Court of Appeal in New South Wales, in British newspapers and on television.

It was one of the most dramatic examples of press censorship in peacetime in Britain that any journalist could remember. Sir Alastair Burnet, ITN's senior newscaster, informed viewers of *News at Ten* on 30 July 1987, "The following report has been compiled within the restrictions of the Law Lords' judgment". That caused one television reviewer to write that this was "The most chilling remark I have ever heard on British television". The report which followed contained a blank screen on several occasions to show where censorship

was in force.

If the situation for the press was serious, the situation regarding Mr Wright's book was absurd. By now the book had been published in the United States, and the British Government let it be known that they would not try to ban it from being brought into Britain. Not because they did not want to ban it, but because they knew they could not.

So, while all forms of printing or broadcasting of excerpts from the book were banned in Britain, an ITN reporter flew into London Airport with a dozen copies under his arm, and was waved smilingly through Customs.

Meanwhile the book was on sale in the United States, Australia and New Zealand, and was being translated, among other languages, into Swahili, Catalan and Mandarin Chinese.

It had become a farce. The censorship net was now riddled with holes, and the Government admitted it had appointed a committee to look at ways of reforming the act.

A year later, in June 1988, the government produced a White Paper which proposed a radical shake-up of the Official Secrets Act. The "catchall" Section Two was scrapped. But it made *all* disclosures by members or former members of the security services a criminal offence. It meant there could be no more prosecutions for reporting how many lumps of sugar the Government Minister liked in his tea, but it also meant there could be no more Peter Wrights.

Four months later, the Law Lords, taking the commonsense view that the damage had already been done, ruled that the British media were at last free to report extracts from *Spycatcher*.

There is no censorship net in the United States. The Constitution says so. The First Amendment to the Constitution reads, "Congress shall make no law ... abridging the freedom of speech, or of the press." And so the United States has no Official Secrets Act. In fact it has quite the opposite: the Freedom of Information Act, which legally guarantees the American citizen free access to government information. The United States might have got the idea from Sweden, whose 1766 freedom of the press act is the oldest in the world.

The basic principle of the act, in the United States and Sweden, is that the public has the right of access to all official records. In the United States its existence was a vital tool in the hands of the Washington Post journalists Carl Bernstein and Bob Woodward in their exposure of the Watergate scandal.

There have in the past been moves

to water the act down. In 1985 the CIA (Central Intelligence Agency) proposed making it a crime for a government employee to disclose to the press classified information which might be considered damaging to national security. In effect, the CIA wanted a law in the United States similar in scope to Britain's Official Secrets Act.

The *Washington Post* reacted angrily. "We do not have such a broad secrecy law in this country and we don't want one", it wrote. The proposal was later dropped.

But there have been other times when the U.S. administration has reacted as if an Official Secrets Act really did exist. It came perilously close in 1986.

The then director of the CIA, William Casey, was furious about leaks to the press which detailed secret American intelligence gathering operations. He threatened to prosecute *The New York Times, Washington Post, Newsweek, Time magazine*, and the *Washington Times*.

Again, it didn't happen.

Senator Hiram Johnson (1866–1945) will not feature large in any history of the United States. But in a speech to the Senate in 1917 he coined a truism, a statement which time after time has been proved to be absolutely correct: ''The first casualty when war comes is truth.'' For, Official Secrets Act or no Official Secrets Act, law or no law, democracy or dictatorship — when a country goes to war, the government censors its press.

You expect it in the Eastern bloc. I have already mentioned Poland. It was no different when I tried to report the Soviet invasion of Afghanistan. I could hardly expect daily press briefings from the Soviets! What I got, once again, was arrest and deportation. The truth was simply too dangerous to be allowed out.

But the world's great democracies can be guilty too.

In 1983 the United States invaded the Caribbean island of Grenada. The press were excluded from the operation — the first time the United States had ever kept the press out of a war zone where it was fighting.

The trouble with letting the press in on a war, is that journalists often learn things of use to the enemy, and it is the authorities' abiding fear that they will publish them.

When Britain went to war on a small group of islands in the South Atlantic called the Falklands Islands, it, as the United States was to do a year later, gagged the Press. It was less of a gag, in that reporters went on board the

Task Force, and went to the Islands, but it was, in a sense, all the more frustrating in that the British authorities controlled the lines of communication. Television pictures, telexes, telephone lines from that distant place 8,000 miles from Fleet Street were all controlled by the British forces, and when they did not want the news to get out, or when they did not like what the reporters were saying, they simply did not let the news reach home.

For instance, no television coverage exists of the central engagements of the War — Goose Green, Bluff Cove, and so on — because news cameras were kept away. The British public knew only such details of the first war its soldiers had fought for more than 40 years as were given out by a dry government official each day in Whitehall.

Democracies, in war and peace, censor news.

White South Africa is a democracy, in the sense that it holds free elections. (However, as long as the majority black population do not have the right to vote, the country cannot be called a true democracy.) South Africa too exercises press censorship.

On 12 June 1986 after growing unrest in the black townships, the South African Government declared a state of emergency.

The state of emergency forbids the press from reporting on any unrest.

In May 1987 Britain's two Johannesburg-based television correspondents, Peter Sharp and Michael Buerk, were expelled from South Africa for contravening the state of emergency regulations. They had both filmed and transmitted to London scenes of unrest and police action at universities in Cape Town and Johannesburg. The complete scenes were not shown on South African television.

France and West Germany are both democracies. Neither censors the news. Yet when the Government changes, so do the editors of the state-run television news organizations.

Britain is a democracy, yet the BBC has had a number of run-ins with the Government. In 1985 a BBC programme containing an interview with a suspected member of the outlawed IRA was stopped by the BBC's governors, after complaints from the Government. The action led to a strike by BBC journalists. The programme was eventually screened.

Two years later the BBC planned to show a documentary about a secret spy satellite codenamed 'Zircon'. There were rows in Parliament, and

Scotland Yard Special Branch officers raided the BBC's offices in Scotland. The programme was withdrawn, although a year later the BBC, under its new management, announced that it would be screened.

In May 1988, the British Government had less success. After three IRA terrorists were shot dead by security forces in Gibraltar, both the BBC and ITV made programmes including interviews with eye-witnesses to the shootings.

The British Government asked both networks to postpone their programmes until after the inquest into the deaths was held in Gibraltar. They both refused and, to the Government's anger, the programmes were shown.

But in October of that year, the British Government did act against the broadcasters: it imposed a ban on radio and television interviews with any terrorist organization *or its supporters*. This barred interviews with Sinn Fein, the political wing of the IRA,

Watch for the caption in TV news bulletins: Official Government Film.

one of whose leaders was a democratically elected Member of Parliament.

Press are used to censorship from the Eastern bloc. In the Gorbachev era, though, the foreign journalist has found censorship considerably eased. Twice a week now there is a press briefing at the Ministry of Foreign Affairs in Moscow. A chief foreign affairs spokesman has been appointed, with the job of answering questions from the foreign press. An impossibility before Gorbachev came to power. Television crews can work in the streets of the city relatively free from police interference or without having to get their reports past a censor.

The relationship between governments and the press is a love-hate relationship. Governments will want their successes reported, but not their failures. Journalists will want to know things the governments won't want them to know. Neither can stop the other existing. They just have to learn to live together.

What do you think might be the effect of having TV editors appointed by the government? Could the news be unbiased? Could the news criticize the government?

"REVEAL YOUR SOURCES"

In a democracy, of course, everyone is subject to the law. And if a journalist coexists with the government, he must also coexist with the law. Most will go through their careers with no greater brush with the law than a ticket for parking on a double yellow line while chasing a story.

Of all the laws, the threat of **libel** (publishing a false statement about someone which may damage their reputation) is perhaps the most ever-present legal constraint on the journalist. It is not for nothing that journalists make such liberal use of the word *alleged* in their copy.

But there is one aspect of the law which journalists will join ranks to defy, and for which defiance they will readily risk a prison sentence: the refusal to reveal their sources.

To a journalist the relationship he has with a **source** is a sacred trust. The principle is simple: the source will give the journalist information in return for anonymity. The source may have any number of reasons for remaining anonymous. He may lose his job if it becomes known that he has passed sensitive information to a journalist. Depending on how sensitive it is, he may even lose his life.

The journalist will maintain that anonymity, of course, because he would not want to harm his source; but also because if he broke the bargain, the source would "dry up".

Most journalists most of the time have no difficulty in protecting the identity of their sources. The difficulty arises when the information passed to the journalist by the source concerns national security, or the possibility of a crime having been committed.

British courts have always claimed that they respect the right of the journalist to protect his sources. To make the journalist's legal position clearer, that principle was given the force of law in 1981.

The law is the Contempt of Court Act 1981. The relevant part is section ten, and it states, "No court may require a person to disclose, nor is any person guilty of contempt of court for refusing to disclose, the source of information contained in a publication for which he is responsible, *unless it is established to the satisfaction of the court that disclosure is necessary in the interests of justice or national security, or for the prevention of disorder or crime.*" (My emphasis.)

It sounds plain enough, but it is that

Read a newspaper, or watch a news programme and note how many stories quote *unofficial* or *informed* sources.

second part in italics that causes the problems, because it raises these questions: What if the journalist disagrees with the court over its criteria for the interests of justice or national security, or over its criteria for the prevention of disorder or crime? And what if he still refuses to disclose the source of his information, despite the court ruling?

Take first the question of national security. This was tested in 1983 when *The Guardian* newspaper in Britain received, unsolicited, a photocopy of a Ministry of Defence document concerning the arrival in Britain of American Cruise missiles — an extremely delicate issue at the time. The paper published the document, the Government took legal action, and the court ordered *The Guardian* to return the copy to the Government.

The reason the Government wanted the copy back was that it believed the document might reveal the identity of the source, i.e. allow it to establish who had leaked the document to *The Guardian*. The paper realized the motive, of course, and argued in court that under section 10 of the Contempt of Court Act it did not have to return the document.

The argument failed. Such a leak was held to threaten the interests of national security. The newspaper returned the document to the Government. The Government *was* able to establish from the document the source of the leak. She was a Foreign Office clerk named Sarah Tisdall. She was prosecuted under the notorious Section Two of the Official Secrets Act, found guilty and sent to prison for six months.

Equally contentious is the final phrase of section ten, "... *for the prevention of disorder or crime.*"

In 1987 a British financial journalist named Jeremy Warner wrote two articles which were published in two of Britain's leading quality newspapers, *The Times* and *The Independent*. In the articles the journalist made it clear that he had a source inside a Government Department who was leaking to him confidential information about take-over bids. The source told him that this information was also being leaked to people who were using it to speculate on the Stock

Exchange. This kind of operation is known as "insider dealing" and it is illegal.

The Government appointed inspectors to hold an inquiry into the leaks and the insider dealing ring, which involved the sum of £10 million.

Obviously the one person who could tell them a lot that they wanted to know was Jeremy Warner. He refused, claiming that section ten of the Contempt of Court Act afforded him protection against revealing his sources.

But his argument failed. The Court ruled that the purpose of the inquiry was the prevention of crime, and that section ten of the act specifically excluded this from protection.

The journalist accepted the ruling, as he had to — and *still* refused to reveal his sources. As he put it in a newspaper interview, "I'm in an impossible position. Either I reveal my sources and commit professional suicide, or I accept punishment. There is only one real option: to accept punishment".

The case finally came to court in January 1988. The judge accepted the journalist's defence that he genuinely had not intended to break the law. He fined him £20,000. As in most cases like this, the newspaper paid the fine.

Possibly the most famous anonymous source in the history of journalism was Deep Throat, from whom the *Washington Post* journalists Bernstein and Woodward received information that the Watergate affair reached to the very highest level of the United States administration, namely the Oval Office of the President.

To this day only three people know for sure who Deep Throat was: Bernstein, Woodward and Deep Throat himself (herself?).

For the television journalist, revealing your source can have a rather different meaning. In March 1988 two British soldiers were murdered in Northern Ireland in horrific circumstances. They were dragged from their car by a crowd attending a funeral into whose path they had strayed. They were beaten up, stripped and shot.

Even by Northern Ireland standards it was particularly brutal, and a British public already hardened to horror stories from the province was appalled.

Soldiers have been killed before in Northern Ireland, but these murders aroused a greater than usual outcry because the television cameras were there and the brutality was plain to see.

Both ITN and BBC carried the story

on their bulletins — the crowd surging round the car like hounds moving in for the kill, the windows of the car smashed and the soldiers dragged out.

So far so uncontroversial. But two days later the Royal Ulster Constabulary — Northern Ireland's police force — ordered ITN and the BBC to hand over all their video, transmitted and untransmitted, to help them conduct a murder investigation.

Now no television news organisation minds handing over transmitted material, since it is already in the public domain. But untransmitted material is quite another thing. It is, strictly speaking, private property. But there is more to it than that.

ITN's Editor David Nicholas summed it up like this: "ITN's role is to inform the public. Its ability to cover the news, particularly in Northern Ireland, would be jeopardised if its untransmitted material were to be readily available to the police".

In other words, how could our news people work on the streets of Belfast, when the crowds there knew that any film shot could be handed over to the police at their request? It would, at best, mean filming was impossible, and at worst put the crew's lives at risk.

Predictably, then, both ITN and the

BBC refused to comply with the police order. There was an outcry. More than 100 members of Parliament signed a motion expressing disbelief at the broadcasters' refusal. And the Prime Minister Mrs Thatcher said in the House of Commons: "Either one is on the side of justice in these matters or on the side of terrorists".

That was, in the broadcasters' view, an unfair statement, particularly since they wanted very much to abide by the law. In fact Mr David Nicholas' statement ended by saying: "ITN does not consider itself to be above the law and it is open to the authorities to use the due process of the law in its inquiries".

In other words, you can force us by law to hand over our pictures, and we will comply. But we must be seen to be forced by law to do something which we will not do in answer to a simple request.

And that is what happened. The police invoked three laws: the Prevention of Terrorism Act, The Northern Ireland Criminal Law Act, and the Northern Ireland Emergency Powers Act. And they threatened the broadcasters with arrest if they refused.

The broadcasters, albeit with a heavy heart, handed over their untransmitted material. In television terms, they "revealed their sources".

If you interviewed a criminal and the police asked you to reveal his identity and whereabouts, would you do it?

THE INTERVIEW

You could be on television tomorrow. You might be the sole witness to a major bank robbery or a disaster.

Of all the different kinds of interview you will see on the television news, the eye-witness interview is the easiest to do and the least controversial.

The reporter is seeking information, and all you have to do is give it. If you want to. Anyone can walk away from a television camera, but in practice the eye-witness to a dramatic event will be eager to tell his story. Also because he knows that in this kind of case the reporter will not be challenging him, or trying to put him on the spot.

What the reporter will be looking for is what is called in the United States a **sound-bite**: a clear succinct capsule of information, told in as short a time as possible. I once heard the ultimate sound-bite on American television. A single word. "No". But usually a sound-bite will run from about 10 seconds to around 30 seconds, rarely more.

From your point of view, it's easy. Just tell it like it was.

In Britain there is no law of privacy.

In other words, you cannot take action against a reporter who you may consider has "hounded" you. But television news editors set themselves certain standards. For instance, my own company, ITN, will not show scenes of intense personal grief. If someone breaks down while being interviewed, we will not show it. If tears start to flow, the cameraman will not zoom in to see it in tight close-up. If he does, we will not broadcast it. The rule by which we operate is: we will not intrude on personal grief.

Political interviews can be very difficult. In the early days of television, the political interview as we know it today simply did not exist. There is a marvellous clip in the archives of British television news, showing a reporter putting a microphone under a Government Minister's mouth and asking: "Minister, would you be so kind as to make a statement for our viewers?" "Certainly," the Minister replied, and turning straight to the camera, made his statement, secure in the knowledge that he would not be questioned or challenged.

A reporter conducting an interview along those lines today would not last a week in the business.

Today a politician being interviewed for television knows that he will be challenged on his position, no matter what political view he represents. The role of the reporter is to take the position of the viewer. What questions would the viewer like to be answered?

The politician, of course, knows what he wants to say, and he will make sure he says it, whatever you ask him!

Often, if a politician wants to make a particular point, he will *offer* himself for interview. This immediately makes the journalist wary. He does not like his programme to be used simply as a "platform" for the politician's views. In a case like this, whether the news editor will agree to the politican being interviewed will depend solely on the strength of the story.

There is a technical point to bear in mind about the television news interview, which politicians are especially wary about. Barring exceptional occasions, it is always shot with a single camera. And that camera is always on the interviewee.

That is fine. But if that is how it is done, you might ask, how come you often see the interviewer asking the questions? The answer is that after the interview, the reporter asks the questions again, this time with the camera on him. These questions are called **cut-aways**, or **cut-ins**, or (in the United States) the **re-asks**.

Identify the re-asks in an interview. Can you tell the questions were added later?

The American word re-asks describes exactly what they are: the questions being asked again. The English words describe exactly what happens to them: the picture editor cuts away from the interviewee and edits in the questions.

Fine and dandy, but consider the opportunity for fraud, for making the reporter look, say, more aggressive than he has in fact been, or the interviewee seem weaker. During the interview, the reporter might have asked: "Are you against the Government on this issue?" When he does the cut-away, he might choose to ask: "You aren't seriously suggesting that yours is a credible alternative to what the Government is proposing, surely?"

The reason an unethical reporter could get away with this is that most politicians are in a rush, and as soon as the interview is over they will hurry away. The reporter is then left alone with his crew to do his cut-aways.

It would, of course, take a pretty unscrupulous reporter to do such a thing (and an equally unscrupulous crew to let him), but it can happen — usually to a lesser degree — by accident.

In Britain a television news reporter going out to do an interview will have only his crew with him; no producer. He will, of course, write a list of questions and have them on his lap during the interview. But a good reporter will never stick to his questions like glue. If the interviewee raises an interesting angle in his answer, the reporter might choose to explore it.

Since he will be listening to the answers very carefully, the reporter might well not want to break his concentration by writing down the question he has just asked. So that when he comes to do his cut-aways, it is possible that he will forget the exact wording of his question. Or he might forget the question altogether. Whatever the reasons, it should not happen. The cut-aways should exactly mirror the original questions, in content and tone.

I know of certain politicians in Britain who will always make sure they do. They bring a secretary into an interview. The secretary will note down every question the reporter asks, *exactly*. The politician will stay and watch the reporter doing his cut-aways, and God help the reporter if he gets a single word wrong!

A reporter is often asked by the person being interviewed to reveal the questions he is going to ask before the interview starts. In some cases the reporter will even be asked to produce a written list of questions. This is something reporters will avoid agreeing to at all costs.

If a reporter does agree, he will feel within his rights to change the questions once the interview gets going. I have had to do this many times and have never been taken to task for doing so.

The only exception to this might be when interviewing a member of the public, when warning them of your questions in advance can put them at their ease.

Once you have given an interview, is there anything you can do to influence the way it is used? In a word, no.

In practice, the skilled interviewees (which usually means politicians, because they do it so often) have their own techniques.

The first I have already mentioned. If a politician wants to make a particular point, he will make it, no matter what you ask him. The usual technique will be:

Reporter: Do you believe the Government will cut public spending?

Politician: Before I answer that, let me make it perfectly clear that . . .

This is an example of a politician *using* the media to get his point across. The television journalist hates this, but it is a necessary evil. At least the reporter can challenge the politician with his next question. And the public are becoming increasingly aware of politicians "soapboxing".

Another technique — also a favourite with politicians — is to slide sentences together to make it more difficult to edit. An example of this is:

Politician: The Government must do all in its power to (pause) cut public spending and let me add that it must also (pause) rethink its budget proposals because . . . (He can now go on for ever safe in the knowledge that it will be impossible to edit after the words "public spending".

But most politicians know that television is too useful a medium to abuse it too often. In fact many now practise the exact opposite of what I've just described. They know that if they can give the reporter a perfect (which means short and pithy) soundbite, it is much more likely to get on the air than a long rambling answer.

Look carefully at interviews with politicians. See if they use any of these techniques.

How far can a reporter go in his questioning, and remain within the bounds of decency?

In 1987 when Gary Hart was struggling to remain a Presidential candidate despite allegations that he had had an affair with a model, he gave a press conference. A reporter asked him: "Mr Hart, have you ever committed adultery?"

There was a public outcry at the journalist's audacity. The reporter had asked the one question the public wanted to hear answered. Had the reporters stayed within the bounds of decency? There are no absolute rights or wrongs. You must judge for yourself.

How far should a reporter let his personal views, or bias, intrude on an interview? Not one little bit!

"YOU'RE BIASED!"

Of all the accusations that at one time or another the television journalist will have flung at him, there are two above all which will strike fear into his heart.

The first is: "You got your facts wrong". Say this to a journalist — any kind of journalist — and watch his jaw drop and the look of fear creep across his eyes. It is, of course, an inexcusable sin for a journalist to get his facts wrong.

But this is an easy complaint to deal with, for the simple reason that a fact is a fact is a fact. If a reporter describes the United States as having 48, 49 or 51 States, then that is wrong. The United States has, as a matter of fact, 50 States.

If a reporter gets a title wrong, or a date wrong, or — potentially much more disastrous—wrongly attributes an action or statement to somebody, then he is guilty of factual error. Trivial or not trivial, every fact cited by a journalist must be accurate. And if he is accused of getting a fact wrong, it is usually easily checked with a single phone call to the cuttings library.

But how do you check **bias?**

Examine the differences between your own beliefs, prejudices and biases. For example: in politics, racial matters, your attitude to women's rights, and so on. Honestly!

Because this is the second accusation the reporter dreads: "That report you did was biased".

Let's first define the term. My dictionary defines bias thus: "inclination, predisposition (towards), prejudice, influence".

Don't you agree there is something slightly sinister about all those words? They all have this in common: they imply beliefs or judgments reached *despite* the facts. And you will notice that two words missing from the dictionary's definition of "bias" are "belief" and "judgment". They are innocent words. The others are not.

When is a belief or judgment a bias? When, despite showing someone that the facts belie what he is saying, he still says: "Never mind the facts, I'm sticking to what I say".

And that is why journalists dread the accusation: because it flies in the face of the *facts*, and facts are the tools of his trade.

So, to return to the question I posed a little earlier, how do you check bias? You can't, that is the trouble; that is what makes it all the more sinister.

How then can the journalist avoid it? Not easily, is the glib answer. I once fell into conversation with a young man on a train journey from Manchester to London. We were discussing bias in television news.

"You're all biased," he said. I laughed at the absurdity of his generalisation. Then he said, "When you do a report, every word you choose to use betrays a bias."

Again I laughed off his outrageous remark, but a few weeks later an incident happened which made me think again about whether or not he had been entirely wrong.

I was in Rhodesia, in the final months before independence and its rebirth as Zimbabwe. The Prime Minister was Ian Smith, who some years before had made a Unilateral Declaration of Independence (UDI) from Britain, an act which was regarded by the British Government as nothing less than traitorous.

Ian Smith had just flown home from a trip to the United States, in which he had tried to win backing for his stand against black majority rule and independence. The trip had not been the success he had hoped, because President Carter had refused to see him.

At the airport on his return he held a press conference. I had a question ready, and a follow-up question. (A reporter always has a follow-up question ready, because it can often yield more than the original question.) I put my question to Mr Smith: "How can you hope for international support for your regime, if you are unable even to get to see the American President?" "Why do you call my Government a regime?", he asked. I stuttered and stumbled and mumbled. (The danger of having a follow-up question is that if the answer is not what you expect, you may not be able to switch your train of thought quickly enough.)

This was not only an answer I had not expected, it was an answer I had never dreamed of. (Added to that, it was put in the form of a question. If a politician wants to wrong-foot a reporter, he will often do it by throwing a question back. It has the dual advantage for the politician of putting the onus back on the reporter, as well as evading the question.)

After the press conference, one of Mr Smith's aides came up to me and said: "The trouble with you British reporters is you're all biased against us".

Although my dictionary defines regime simply as "a method or system of government", there is no denying that the modern connotation of the word is slightly different. It implies a level of illegality, or at least of something being not quite right. We don't talk of the "government" of Idi Amin in Uganda, or of Papa Doc Duvalier in Haiti. We use the word "regime". Conversely, we don't talk of the "regime" of Mrs Thatcher in Britain or of President Mitterrand in France.

So Ian Smith had a point. In British eyes he may have been heading a "regime," but in his eyes he was certainly heading a "government", and by using the word "regime" I was loading my question.

Other words hold similar traps for journalists. When is a man a "terrorist" and when is he a "freedom fighter" or a "guerrilla"?

These are problems that journalists have to face every day, and on which they have to make decisions. One way journalists can look at it is this: when opponents of a governing power engage that power's armed forces in combat, they are guerrillas. When they go further than that and bomb indiscriminately, they are terrorists. But there will always be those who argue that journalists are making biased judgements — one person's freedom fighters are another person's terrorists.

You could try to think of more examples.

Some other examples; "Striking miners *wielding* clubs and sticks" is emotive. "Striking miners *carrying* clubs and sticks" is not. "Police armed with batons and riot shields *tore into* the picket lines" is emotive. "Police armed with batons and riot shields *charged* into the picket lines" is not.

An answer, I hope, is beginning to emerge to the question, how does the journalist avoid bias? It is: by sticking to the facts. When challenged, the *facts* are the last refuge of the reporter. Facts need no embellishment.

In 1986 the British Government attacked the BBC for bias. The occasion was the American bombing of the Libyan capital, Tripoli. The Government accused the BBC TV News report of, "Uncritical propaganda which enlisted the audience's sympathy for Libya". The BBC's reply was that the report had simply stated the facts, and that the picture had told the story. It is not the complete answer, of course, for the reason that not everybody likes the facts.

Northern Ireland will once again be an example of what I mean. If one side of the sectarian divide commits an atrocity which its own members do not support, then they will not want the facts revealed to the general public. If the reporter nevertheless reports it, they will accuse him of bias, of making it sound worse than it was. The truth is that their judgment, not the reporter's, has been coloured by bias. There is one way a reporter can tell when he has got it right: when both sides accuse him of bias.

ON AIR!

The television journalist's work is short-lived. It goes out into the air, it is viewed at the other end, and that is it.

A television journalist, unlike his newspaper counterpart, cannot collect his written work and stack it on the shelf. He can line up his notebooks there, but his finished scripts are nothing without the picture they accompanied.

Television news programmes such as *World News Tonight* and *News at Ten* are on the air every day. They report today's news. Not yesterday's. Television journalism is immediate. It is *now*.

Often, when going for the crucial interview on a story, a television reporter will be told by the prospective interviewee, "Well yes, alright, you can interview me, but not until tomorrow". That is one of the worst things a television reporter can be told. Tomorrow is rarely ever any good. It is an uncommon story that will live until the next day. The deadline is always the next bulletin.

Deadline. The word a television journalist will live with for the whole of his career.

"Ten seconds to on air ... five, four, three, two, one, up title music, on air, cue John!"

If you like that kind of tension, there is nothing like it in the world. You and your work are being watched by millions of people simultaneously.

I have written about television journalists. But it takes several hundred people to get a television news bulletin on the air. There are the journalists you see; newscasters, correspondents, reporters. There are the journalists you don't see: programme editors, chief writers, writers, copy tasters (who do just that: "taste" the stories, or copy, from agencies as it comes in, to sift from it the interesting stories to cover). There are the technicians: cameramen, sound recordists, and lighting technicians; studio directors, vision mixers, video editors, electronic engineers, scene shifters, canteen staff ...

Every bulletin is difficult to do. But most journalists — and I — would not exchange it for any other job.

One night, after a particularly difficult day, and a thoroughly fraught bulletin, a colleague, slumped in a chair, looked at me and said: "You know, this is no way for a grown man to earn a living".

But he was smiling, and his eyes were sparkling.